All it takes to give a coolly pared-down
room a sense of softness, warmth
and liveability is an injection of
heart-stopping colour and
one or two sublimely
lovely objects. This
is simplicity at its
most relaxed.

Simple interiors are often thought of as minimalist. But while minimalism might make you think of sparsely furnished, lofty rooms with severe, monochrome colour schemes – the sort of spaces that have now become something of a decorating cliché – the simply decorated rooms of the relaxed home have a far warmer and more liveable character. They may have their roots in minimalism insofar as they are free of clutter and their decorative elements are usually of the pared-down variety, but they are nevertheless gently mellow places where softness and comfort are key, places where people feel a sense of welcome.

But there is more to this look than merely a reaction to minimalism. The beauty of relaxed simplicity lies in the fact that you have the opportunity to soften the minimalism and inject your own sense of individuality into a room by introducing one or two things you are passionate about – maybe an

add shocking pink for bold contrast

opposite In a simple
bedroom where
cushions take the
place of a headboard,
colour is the focal
point. One shocking
pink Chinese silk
cushion adds sparkling
contrast to an
otherwise cool blue
and white scheme.

below left and right
Magenta orchids are
the only adornment on
an uncluttered
dressing table.

exotically coloured fabric or a richly textured throw – without spoiling
the look's characteristic unfussiness. So when you fall in love with that
piece of pink Chinese silk, you can feel free to make it into a cushion
cover and display it as a splash of colour against a plain, white-
upholstered daybed. You can soften the lines of an unpainted wooden
chair by draping it with a length of beautifully muted vintage floral fabric.

Relaxed simplicity relies on having something in every room that
is personal and well loved, something that makes a statement and
gives the room impact. What are the objects that bring you
happiness? Which are the colours that make your heart sing?
What makes you feel at ease? You may choose something with
an appealing texture, something strikingly coloured or attractively
patterned. But the crucial thing to remember is that, to keep the look
simple, you only need one, or two at the most, of these decorative
items. Use more and the spell will be broken.

above left Touches of pink and lilac warm up a simple – verging on the stark – living room. The fifties armchair and surfboard-design coffee table give the space a wonderfully retro feel.

above right Tall floor-to-ceiling windows allow daylight to flood into the room. The airy look is enhanced by pale wood floorboards and tiles. Although the furnishings are the embodiment of simplicity, the room still feels welcoming.

As for the other elements you introduce into the room, bear in mind the fact that the style of furniture you choose is hugely important to the look. The good news though is that relaxed rooms do not require expensive furniture. In fact, an old sofa, junk-shop table or second-hand shop or laboratory fittings will be more at home in this environment than a priceless antique crystal chandelier or a refined gilt and marble console table.

But whether you are starting completely from scratch or furnishing a room with items you already own, the secret of creating simple relaxed rooms is to choose pieces with an almost skeletal quality – those that are characterized by slender, linear shapes and clean lines rather than bold, chunky styles. Think fifties tables on narrow tapering legs or graceful, slightly spare-looking armchairs with plain, unfussy wooden feet. These pieces not only look crisp and streamlined, but also show the maximum amount of floor space underneath and around – an important factor given that a sense of spaciousness is another of the qualities to aim for.

As for colour, it is a powerful decorating tool. It can bring a sense of unity to a busy room or can contribute an essential burst of vitality to a room that is lacking in interest. You also probably want to use a favourite colour in your home, a colour that evokes many memories and emotions for you. However, since the advent of minimalism, you might imagine that simple rooms should only be decorated in pure white or neutral shades such as cream, stone, taupe or parchment. But you will find that, with care, it is perfectly possible to use really bright colours in relaxed simple rooms without compromising the rooms' innate simplicity.

Once you have decided on your favourite colour, consider painting it on just one wall. Surround it with lots of white on the woodwork and even on the floors, then leave the wall free of pictures so as not to detract from the colour's decorative quality. In this way, the colour itself will become your favourite thing, your focal point in the midst of otherwise pared-down, unadorned surroundings. And what could be simpler than that?

soften those classic fifties lines with flowers and fabric

above In a distinctly minimalist corner of a room, the fluid, organic lines of a modern classic chair of moulded plywood are decoration enough. To appreciate the chair fully, all the other decorative elements – the earthy tone of the walls and the bare wooden floorboards – are kept as low-key as possible.

right Contrast is the secret here, as the strong, dark lines of the hand-crafted wooden vase and bowls throw the pure-white-painted fireplace into relief. Such dramatic arrangements – based on just one or two of the owner's favourite things – are a quick and simple way to transform an unexciting room.

this page The owner of this old Parisian apartment exposed the original beams to add textural and visual interest to the plain white walls of an otherwise simple bedroom.

left, above Create a blissfully simple still life by displaying two old glass bottles alongside some scrap metal collected for its colour and textural interest. Soften the scheme by adding a length of old white linen draped along the mantelshelf.

left, below A worn old denim jacket and a fine pashmina shawl hanging against a plain white wall create a visual feast with a wonderfully relaxed and unusually transient quality.

relaxed
romantic

Paint a room in the coolest ice-
cream colours, furnish it with the
simplest beds and chairs, add a
restrained helping of sun-faded
floral fabrics, beads and flowers
and you have the recipe for
today's relaxed romance.

Twenty years ago, if you had asked a designer to create a romantic interior, the chances are you would have ended up with a mass of period frills, flounces and flowers. These frothy, visually complex schemes are the antithesis of modern, pared-down interiors, so it might surprise you to find that romanticism plays a role in today's relaxed homes.

But there is, of course, a crucial difference. Relaxed romanticism takes a conventionally romantic touch – a floral fabric, a beaded throw or a soft pastel paint shade – and places it in a restrained, often minimalist setting. The result is a distillation of conventional romanticism, producing a thoroughly modern feel that is at home in any room in the house.

Femininity and theatricality are both part of the mood. Now is definitely the time to give free rein to all those girly decorative touches you thought were well and truly out of bounds in the contemporary home. That thirties dress or drop-dead gorgeous kimono that caught your eye at a flea market can become part of your decorating scheme rather than something you end up stowing away in a

One of the most beautiful ways of adding a dash of romance and pattern to any pared-down room is to introduce some delicate floral material, preferably on a white or off-white background. You could try using a flowery throw over the arm of a plain chair or sofa, or one or two dainty floral-patterned cushions to soften the look of a modern steel bed. The bedroom is the ideal place to introduce a piece of vintage clothing. No matter that it is never worn, a floral fifties evening dress draped casually over a dressing-table stool readily becomes part of the room's decoration.

nothing could be more romantic

than floral fabrics

in the bedroom

wardrobe. It doesn't matter if you never wear them; owning them and showing them off is satisfying in itself. Display them on sturdy wooden hangers against a wall like works of art, and change them with the seasons or according to your mood.

Costume jewellery and theatrical-looking accessories can serve as decoration, too. Strands of glittery beads and pretty necklaces look fabulous draped over the corner of a picture frame; a pile of brooches in a glass dish might be the only adornment a plain white-painted mantelpiece needs; a collection of glamorously sexy satin shoes can be turned into a focal point with a difference; a cane mannequin generously festooned with necklaces becomes an object of desire, especially when it is standing on a delicate gilded metal console table.

See how a beautifully tactile lilac beaded throw can soften the effect of a white-painted table and how a number of different fabrics – jacquards, floral prints and quilted cottons – in closely related shades have more impact when used together. A simple bunch of flowers adds a touch of romance.

Flowery fabrics, once spurned for being over-sentimental, are again big news, and many textile manufacturers have re-issued old designs to capture the new romantic mood. This time around, though, the look is altogether fresher and simpler. The trick is to use restraint. A flowery cushion cover or a single chair covered in informal, blowsy-looking chintz are all you need. Choose soft and simple colourways, preferably with a white or neutral background, and make sure that the rest of the room is not fighting for attention. Walls should be painted in neutral colours or soft pastels; furniture should have simple, uncomplicated lines.

Nostalgia for the past immediately conjures up romance and so is another key influence in relaxed romantic. Wherever you can, use sun-faded fabrics, old-fashioned alarm clocks, saggy sofas, roll-top baths and old

shine on in gilt, glass and satin

cut-glass vases instead of their modern equivalents. But whereas twenty years ago it would have been de rigueur to display these items in rooms decorated in a heavy pastiche of a past style, now they should be set alongside minimalist white walls and white-painted floors.

For in the relaxed romantic interior, freshness, lightness, wit and irreverence have replaced slavish co-ordination and tired old historical clichés. Romance is there at every turn, but this newly minted version is sparkling, lively and never over-sentimental.

above left
Surround yourself with your favourite things. These drop-dead gorgeous shoes have an almost sculptural quality when arranged on an old gilded screen.

above centre For a display that allows you to revel in the quintessential romance of florals, simply leave a flower-encrusted evening bag lying on a chintz-covered armchair.

above right A wicker dressmaker's dummy draped with quirky costume jewellery prevents a gilded table and mirror from appearing over-formal.

opposite An assortment of vintage beads and costume jewellery bought at fairs and markets introduces elements of theatricality and nostalgia as well as romance.

relaxed
sensuality

When you long to indulge your senses of sight, smell and touch, choose relaxed sensuality and surround yourself with a wealth of richly varied colours, fabrics, shapes, textures and patterns.

opposite Rumpled yet luxurious. Richly embroidered bedlinen and satin pillowslips epitomize today's relaxed sensuality.

left In relaxed rooms, furniture and accessories do not always have to be used for the purpose for which they were intended. Here a sari hangs at the window to diffuse the light and cast a richly coloured glow. The sensual effect is heightened by its juxtaposition with the clinical – white-painted floorboards, a retro-style chrome trolley and lamp, and an old-style radiator.

above (inset) A bed below a sunny window is the perfect spot for an afternoon nap. Yet again, the sensuous element – a gold-embroidered cushion cover – contrasts sharply with the austere – the crisp white bedlinen beneath.

freshly
fuchsia

left An intricate earring artlessly laid on a mantelshelf demonstrates how the unexpected can become part of your interior decoration.

opposite, left The details are simple but the effect is sensuous. Create it yourself with layers of rich colours for bedding, wall hangings and even book covers. Use shades of hot pink, red and orange for a sense of enveloping warmth and comfort.

opposite, right Tactile embroidered and ruched fabrics look even more spectacular alongside dainty florals.

Relaxed simplicity and relaxed romantic are characterized by the beauty of their restraint. Their hallmark is their specially selected decorative touches here and there amid otherwise fairly low-key surroundings. There may be times, however, when you feel like being a little less self-disciplined, when you long to indulge yourself and create a more complex interior. Rather than limiting yourself to one or two tasteful objects in a room, you might yearn to include a profusion of your favourite things.

Think relaxed sensuality and you immediately have a theme that, with the greatest subtlety, will provide the link you need to bring all the different elements together. With relaxed sensuality, you can not only appeal to the sense of sight, but also to the senses of touch and smell. Relaxed sensuality gives you the excuse to introduce more than one colour to a room, to put a rich array of patterns next to one another, to mix contrasting textures, even to capitalize on the scent of seasonal flowers to add atmosphere. Decorate a whole house like this and it will be overbearing, but make just one room especially sensual, the rest restrained, and the contrast will prove stunning.

right The simplest touches – sunshine and fresh air coming in at an open window and a jam jar of delicate bluebells on the table – are enough to boost your sense of wellbeing and make you feel your senses are being pampered.

opposite, above For extra sensory richness, feast your eyes on small indulgences such as coloured hand-painted glassware and vividly patterned ceramics.

opposite, below Use sensuous details sparingly and they will have even more impact. Fresh flower-heads heaped on a plate bring a splash of colour to a room as well as sweet fragrance. Choose beautiful orchids for out-and-out exoticism.

Start by indulging the sense of sight – the most important of the five senses for interior decorating. Introduce a riot of deep colours – sexy pinks, burnt umbers, sultry purples or exotic turquoises. Let saturated blues and greens transport you to the seaside.

Introduce these colours on walls, then enrich the visual feast with an assortment of throws, curtains, cushions, lamps and flowers. Combine closely related tints – think ochre and brown with terracotta or shocking pink, brick red with burnt orange – to give a room a feeling of intimacy. Or put together vividly contrasting shades – turquoise with lilac or cerise, lime green with orange – to surprise and revitalize.

With relaxed sensuality you can happily put rich textures against this vibrant backdrop, so keep this in mind when selecting everything from fabrics and flooring to furniture and work surfaces. Introduce ceramic tiles, marble, wood, brick or metal. Go to town with a range of fabrics that feel wonderfully sensuous – silks and satins, velvets, cashmere, suede and tweed. And since textured materials have their own inherent patterns, by using them you will be appealing to the sense of sight as well as to the sense of touch.

As for the sense of smell, it is well known that scent and sensuality go hand in hand. If you do not have honeysuckle growing outside your window or a tangy sea breeze wafting in through an open door, then improvise with a vase of perfumed fresh flowers, a bowl of rose petals or a smouldering incense stick.

Once you start to nourish your senses you will quickly realize how they can add another dimension to your life. So harness their power and bring them into every room of the house with relaxed sensuality.

relaxed elegance

Put a lavish carved bed in an understated bedroom, a fifties glass vase in a grand hallway and you have relaxed elegance – the grown-up, glamorous face of today's relaxed living.

Relaxed elegance has an underlying glamour. It is the grown-up face of relaxed living – the style to adopt if you want a hint of formality. Tailor-made for lofty rooms with high ceilings, moulded cornices and generous windows, relaxed elegance is opulent but modern and measured, so it can be surprisingly effective in contemporary settings, too.

The look begins with the main items of furniture and for relaxed elegance you need one or two breathtaking pieces. It will pay you to look around second-hand shops and antique markets. If you are lucky enough to find an intricately carved turn-of-the-century wooden bed, for example, you will transform an ordinary bedroom into a ravishing boudoir.

unique period pieces set the tone but are not overpowering

Relaxed elegance demands an injection of grandeur and glamour in otherwise simple, contemporary rooms. In this bedroom, highly polished floorboards speak of traditional country-house sophistication in a way that bleached or colourwashed boards would not. A classic carved French bed draped with luxury fabrics and a big vase of freshly gathered flowers continue the theme. Notice how the bed's carving is the room's only concession to ornament and how the plainness of its surroundings emphasizes its intricacy.

In the same way, an original seventies sofa and matching chairs will bring a touch of class to a living area, while a single gilded chair will give even the most modest corner ideas above its station. And you can never go wrong with a daybed or chaise longue – both are the epitome of elegant self-indulgence. Splash out on one or two pieces like these and they will do most of the hard work for you, creating a sense of glamour at a stroke. Meanwhile, keep the rest of the furniture simple to ensure that understatement rules and the balance does not tip towards ostentation.

plain and simple backdrops offset by lavish accessories

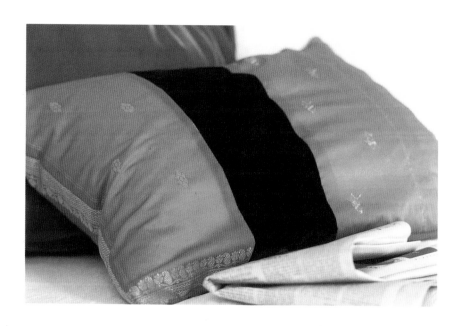

To prevent relaxed
elegance from
becoming over-the-top
opulence, the secret
is to keep the backdrop
clean and simple.
With off-white walls
and woodwork and
understated yet
generously proportioned
sofas, a room can
easily handle a dramatic
gilded mirror, an ornate
period wall clock and
piles of cushions
covered in velvets
and sari silks.

right and opposite, left There is no need to feel that elegance can only be found in conventional 'period' pieces. Items from the sixties are now enjoying a comeback and appear in the relaxed home in many different guises. Here a couple of pieces of vivid retro glassware make a surprisingly successful combination with a more traditionally elegant console table and mirror. The idea of juxtaposing the unusual continues with the addition of a modern, unframed black and white photograph.

opposite, right Mantelpiece arrangements do not have to follow a conventional formula either. An elegant period teacup with a modern glass vase in clashing colours is altogether less formal.

Decorate using colours associated with the elegance of past ages – a palette of delicate *eau de nil*, olive, cream and dreamy sky blue – then continue the elegant theme with sumptuous fabrics; ultra-soft velvets or chunky corduroys on everything from armchairs to cushion covers and generously draped window treatments. Alternatively, use lighter weight fabrics, but in abundance. Muslin curtains flowing on to the floor in generous folds or chairs swathed in yards of linen are less costly but still look lavish. And instead of gentle florals, choose plain, sophisticated fabrics in light shades.

Complement everything with polished parquet or floorboards and elegant lighting. Delicately shaded and gilded wall lights or second-hand crystal chandeliers, perhaps with painted rather than gilded brackets, make just the right statement.

Finally, underline the mood with your choice of accessories. A gently ticking antique clock on an otherwise empty mantelpiece, a fine glass vase filled with orchids on a decorative metal side table, a soft pashmina shawl used as a throw – all these small touches add understated opulence. Feel the glamour, but stay cool – and always utterly relaxed.

relaxed
eclectic

Flaunt your magpie instinct and make the most of the relaxed home's laid-back and wholly unassuming backdrop by embellishing it with beautiful displays of all the things you love.

right Old fabrics tend to have lots of character. Their faded colours and soft, worn texture mean that they are very much at home in a relaxed interior.

far right and opposite, below Combine elements from around the world to create rooms that are truly eclectic. A decorative bottle or the simplest oriental dish and lacquered chopsticks add a touch of the exotic.

opposite, above The contents of your wardrobe are bound to reflect your character and passions. With relaxed eclectic, you can put it all on show and make it part of your room's decor. It does not matter if you have a penchant for shoes, a craving for vintage clothing or a thirst for ethnic pieces, they will all help project your individuality.

geisha girl and english rose

make a heady mixture

In today's fast-moving world the media is constantly bombarding us with all the latest trends in fashion and interior decoration. While it is relatively inexpensive to keep up with fashion fads and change the look of one's wardrobe every season or so, it is a different matter when it comes to decorating our homes. Who but the very rich can afford a complete decorating makeover the minute interior designers decree that minimalism is out and retro is in?

Many people's taste cannot be neatly pigeon-holed in the way that some designers would like. Most of us find a variety of widely differing looks appealing and often cannot choose between them. If this describes you, then relaxed eclectic could be just what you are looking for.

Forget the confusion and clutter that often result when you try to bring together furnishings and fabrics in different styles or personal bits and pieces whose only unifying feature is the fact that you like them, for in the relaxed home – where the backdrop is simple – you can introduce whatever you please without spoiling the visual peace and sense of tranquillity. Do not be worried if your bedroom ends up a mix of English rose and geisha girl, or your sitting room turns into a blend of country cottage and industrial chic, for the very purpose of relaxed eclecticism is to cross many boundaries and juxtapose the unexpected.

So where might you find inspiration? Your travels could well be the starting point. If you have been abroad, you are sure to have brought back some souvenirs. These are supposed to act as reminders of places we

relaxed eclectic

is a collector's dream

have visited but so often, once we are home, they are put away in a drawer or cupboard, then forgotten. With relaxed eclecticism you can take them out, dust them off, and use them as the basis for some chic interior decoration. For instance, banknotes brought home from far-flung corners of the globe make an original display with a few photographs and other memorabilia, or pieces of ethnic fabric can be brought together on a pinboard or in a cluster of mismatched frames.

Places you dream of but may never have visited can also spark off a stream of ideas. Be inspired by the sun-drenched deco colours of Miami or Morocco, by the bold floral fabrics of Haiti or by a collection of delicate Chinese paper lanterns.

If you collect like a magpie, your collections can also be a starting point for some relaxed eclectic decoration. You may

Why buy new when retro has far more character? If you love shopping at junk shops, flea markets and antique stalls, do not hide your purchases away in a cupboard. The relaxed eclectic approach to decorating means that you can put your finds on show without your home ending up looking like a museum.

The secret is to keep to a neutral, unifying backdrop – understated walls and floors – then furniture and accessories from different eras will look good together. The owner of this house has succesfully combined pieces from the fifties and sixties with a collection of modern, hand-thrown vases.

below Furniture and accessories from the fifties have clean, simple lines that give a sense of air and space to a room. Here a classic fifties sofa on tapered wooden legs is flanked by a pair of laminate-topped Scandinavian-style side tables and two unusual lamps of the period. The floor is of polished wooden boards and the brick wall has been painted white.

have cupboards full of vintage clothing, pieces of antique fabric, silk flowers, record covers, retro ceramics, modern paintings, seaside postcards – the possibilities are as endless as your imagination. Show these off on your mantelshelf against simple walls, on a windowsill, in plain picture frames – however seems appropriate.

And if you enjoy collecting artefacts or furniture from different eras – kitsch ornaments from the fifties or seventies furniture – mix and match them for a fresh and unusual take on collecting. Remember that with relaxed eclectic, the aim is not to create a museum-like interior, but one where you can relax and feel completely comfortable. You could even go one step further and mix antique and contemporary, formal and informal, urban and rural. Eclecticism is so

very personal that it offers the opportunity for your own special brand of humour to shine through. So indulge in delightfully whimsical displays or arrangements of objects that verge on the eccentric. Just make sure that they bring a smile to your face and stop you taking either yourself or your sense of style too seriously. And because the look is relaxed, feel free to alter the details whenever you want, adding new treasures to a wall display, propping up a recent discovery on a shelf, replacing a collection of teacups with a row of beautiful shoes. Make an interior that is always evolving and you will never tire of it.

However transient these eclectic decorative touches appear, remember that they are just as much a part of your decor as the paint on the walls and the floorboards. They will prove to be exactly what you need to make your relaxed home truly personal.

below left Relaxed eclectic means surrounding yourself with things that you love. The flowing, organic form of this unique magazine rack more than earns it a place in the room.

below centre Allow your sense of humour free rein. Kitsch salt and pepper shakers prevent a room from becoming over-precious and taking itself too seriously.

below right Unusual juxtapositions are a feature of relaxed eclectic. Here, the linear sixties furniture has been given a surprising injection of feminine comfort in the shape of a floral cushion cover.

relaxed
rooms

living rooms

A warmly welcoming focal point,
generously proportioned sofa,
soothing light and an airy feel –
these are the ingredients that will
make your living room come alive
in a truly relaxing way.

The living room usually sets the tone for the whole house. It is often the first room guests see when they come to visit so you might feel that you have to be on your best behaviour when you decorate it. But if a living room is designed to impress outsiders rather than nurture the people who live there, it will end up feeling contrived, sterile and formal. It will certainly lack the flair and idiosyncrasy that come so easily when your guard is down and you decorate more private spaces such as bedrooms and bathrooms.

The relaxed look should really come into its own in your living area, for this is the place where you come to put your feet up and unwind after a long, hard day. And if you are hoping to turn your entire home into an oasis of easy-going style, the living room is a great place to start.

So what is the secret of creating a relaxed living room? The first is undoubtedly to put something warm and welcoming at its heart. Too often everything in a living room revolves around the television; sofas and chairs are invariably arranged so their occupants can see the screen. The result is a space that is cold and isolating, so break the mould and choose an alternative focus.

If you have the space, a fireplace makes an ideal focal point. In late autumn and winter, fill it with glowing logs or coals. It can continue to be a focal point in warmer weather too; decorate the hearth with a cluster of gently flickering candles. Nor is

left For instant nostalgia, nothing beats the chic combination of a thirties burr walnut table and great accessories such as a retro wireless and an old flexible chrome desk lamp. Attractive yet functional design classics like these can sometimes be found in flea markets, but they are becoming so popular that many companies are now reviving the designs and producing them for a new audience. To complete – and relax – the effect, just add a few flowers in a glass.

A real log fire will always make a living area feel homely and deeply relaxed, even when the fireplace has a strictly minimal design. Intensify the sensuality of the room by filling it with the warm, honey tones of wood, leather and velvet, and by adding accessories such as a mohair and satin throw and some luxurious velvet cushions.

sensual textures
bring life to pale neutrals

there the need to feel that your fireplace has to have a conventional hearth and grate; a simple white-painted wooden fire surround or even a plain unframed wall opening can project a sense of warmth just as much as an ornately carved period mantelpiece. And if you have a mantelshelf, resist the temptation to load it with lots of fussy ornaments. The clean lines of a vase of contorted willow, a few favourite framed pictures propped up on top or a single prized artefact will have far more impact than myriad possessions.

A single particularly beautiful object placed on a side table makes another focal point that can be just as transfixing as the dancing flames in a fireplace. Try a bold, contemporary oil painting propped up on the table, a pile of sea-washed stones collected during a beachcombing expedition, an elegant foliage houseplant or a vase of splendid fresh flowers.

When it comes to the furniture, the sofa is perhaps the most important item of all and for the relaxed look, the more generous and

opposite, left Layer
together a wealth of
sensual textures –
leather, wool, velvet and
satin – to put comfort at
the heart of the relaxed
living room.

**right and opposite,
right** This living room
has many of the
features that help
create a relaxed
ambience. The neutral-
coloured sofa is large
and inviting, especially
as it is covered with
comfortable-looking
cushions and a piece of
cosy sheepskin, and
the large window floods
the space with plenty of
natural light. The airy
feel of the coffee table
and the simple white-
painted rocking chair
prevent the furniture
from appearing heavy.
As a bonus, the view
through the window is
wonderfully peaceful.

above Minimalist rooms can be cold and far from relaxed, so introduce softly muted colours for walls and furniture to counteract this tendency.

above right and opposite
Huge windows and low, skeletal furniture enhance the sense of space in this modern apartment while polished floorboards and a restrained use of textured and patterned fabrics add warmth.

indulgent its proportions, the more comfortable and inviting it will be. Position one to give the best view of a focal point for there is nothing more disconcerting than sitting facing a void. And if you have room for two sofas, so much the better. Arrange them opposite one another to create an ambience that fosters good conversation and gives the room a congenial lived-in feel.

Daybeds or low sofas with a small back and long, welcoming seat – the traditional chaise longue – are variations on the sofa theme. They are perfect for instantly establishing a restful, slightly decadent atmosphere. Examples can be found to suit any interior, whether you are into seventies style, love the sleek lines of contemporary design or delight in the down-at-heel shabby chic look. And the more restful the view from the sofa, the better. During spring and summer, try placing one beside a window so you can look out and

enjoy the sunshine. In autumn and winter, draw it up to the fireplace.

Armchairs are the next item of furniture to consider and in the relaxed home these are at their best when they are large enough to curl up in. Pile on the cushions and place a small stool or table nearby so you can put your feet up if you want. For ultimate flexibility and comfort, beanbags are a great choice. They look stylish and project

an extremely relaxed image. You and your guests will love the feeling of sinking deep into them and having them mould themselves around your body.

However large your furniture, to ensure a sense of space remember to choose as many pieces as possible on legs rather than flush with the floor. And when you are shopping for sofas and chairs, remember to sit on them before you buy. Many pieces are not as comfortable as they look.

As for the material you use to cover your furniture, for a timeless, sensuous effect, choose soft, pliable leather, while for an understated look, opt for simple slipcovers made from plain linen or calico. And if pattern appeals to you, try a floral fabric – faded chintz is a good choice – on a sofa or on just one occasional chair. Many people are afraid of using this traditional fabric with its slightly old-fashioned connotations in a contemporary context. But if you do – and especially if you keep the rest of the room pared down and simple – it will add freshness and buzz as well as a hint of romance.

However, in the relaxed living room, not all your soft furnishings have to be fitted or structured. Elegantly draped fabric or a length of material simply wound around an occasional chair will look just as good as fitted covers. Or introduce a folded woollen throw casually draped over the arm of a chair, or a piece of sheepskin placed on the seat.

retro style
with a very
modern feel

above and below

right An avid collector of sixties memorabilia, the owner of this apartment has successfully created a retro mood. Shiny vinyl flooring, rough linen-effect cupboard fronts, and glass and ceramic dishes and vases give the room textural interest.

right This room with its period window and shutters and traditional chairs could easily have become a historical pastiche. The addition of a sixties laminate-fronted chest of drawers and an Anglepoise lamp makes for a much more relaxed approach to decorating.

combine the

unexpected

and feel free to

express your
personality

above left An inherently simple room is given a sense of relaxed sensuous style thanks to the funky white leather-covered beanbag, the ponyskin rug covering the floor and the woven basket holding logs. The pale turquoise walls prevent a sense of austerity from creeping in.

left and inset above Inject your own personality into a room and make it spring into life by displaying small collections of objects you find particularly appealing.

opposite An eclectic assortment of possessions ensures that the decoration of a living room does not take itself too seriously. Formal classical touches like the plaster medallion sit surprisingly well with black denim upholstery, utilitarian lighting, sensual fabric throws and modern photographs.

Because relaxation is the buzzword, you are bound to need somewhere to perch that cup of tea, the gripping novel you are reading, a vase of flowers or the Sunday papers. Occasional tables serve the purpose but there are other, unconventional possibilities that can establish a more effortlessly casual feel. So instead, try using old trunks, blanket chests, hat boxes or wicker hampers and place them within easy reach of sofas and armchairs.

Whereas most of us decorate our living rooms and position the furniture without ever thinking of changing anything until, perhaps, the next time we decorate, relaxed living means flexibility and movability – the opportunity to change a room's layout whenever we fancy or when we acquire something new. Introduce flexibility and movability into your living areas and they will

exude a feeling of ease and relaxed wellbeing. Furniture on castors is
one way of achieving this effect, so try to include a couple of chairs or
a small table on castors, or even a trolley. Continue the casual theme
– imagine creating the impression that you are simply passing through
and may not be staying long – with pictures propped up on the
mantelshelf instead of hanging against the wall in formal arrangements.
Remember, too, that framed family photographs or other images that
have special meaning for you can decorate a room just as well as a
piece of fine art and such items will also add a more personal note.

Mirrors add light and sparkle to any living room, and the bigger they

This relaxed living room capitalizes on natural colours and a wide range of textures to enhance its sense of comfort and sensuality.

are, the better. In a relaxed room give them the same treatment as pictures; a huge, ornate, gilt-edged mirror, for example, might appear ostentatious hanging in the traditional position over a fireplace. For an even more relaxed – and unexpected – effect, stand it on the floor so it leans against the wall. This will be far more striking and the temporary, makeshift image that it projects will give a sense of faded grandeur that sits very comfortably with the relaxed look.

While we do not have much control over the architectural elements in our living rooms, we can make the most of those we have to ensure that they contribute to the room's sense of relaxed style.

It is often the idiosyncratic details – a humorous printed sign, a collection of dried roots, some sensuously silky cushions – that make a room feel relaxed. A chaise longue is an indulgence. Underline the fact with luxurious suede cushions.

**left and opposite,
above right** This
simple fireplace makes
a welcoming focal point
whatever the season. In
warm weather, its
owner fills the hearth
with candles and puts
fresh garden flowers on
the mantelpiece. The
eclectic display also
includes personal
mementoes collected
over the years.

**opposite, above left
and below right**
Calming shades of
cream, off-white and
beige are used on walls
and woodwork, to
cover the comfortable
sofa and to unify a
collection of china jugs.
A pair of cushions
covered in vivid
Chinese silk and faded
English floral cotton add
a burst of colour and a
gentle touch of
romance.

The secret is to work with, rather than against, such elements. If you adopt this approach, your living room will automatically have a sense of cohesion since everything will be in keeping with the building as a whole.

You might, for instance, have an architectural feature such as wood panelling or a wooden floor and may feel that this is too formal for relaxed living. But you are mistaken. Instead, make the most of it. If a relaxed simple or relaxed romantic look is what you want to achieve, or if you want a clear, neutral backdrop for your possessions, then gently tone the wood down by giving it a coat of light-coloured paint or limewash. Think white, grey, pale green or cream.

Alternatively, if you want some warmth

Old luggage is easy to find (and often affordable) and makes an unusual place to stand a mirror and a plant, or rest the morning paper and a cup of tea.

underfoot, you could cover your wooden floor with natural jute. For a more elegant but still relaxed feel, buff up the wood with wax polish to reveal its textural qualities and subtle colour. Darker woods such as oak and old pine have mature, rich tones and a beautiful grain. They make the perfect setting for one or two very special and unique pieces of classic furniture.

If you are fortunate, your living room will have large windows and be flooded with natural light. Plenty of sunshine is perhaps the greatest asset any room can have, so revel in it by avoiding fussy curtain treatments that will shut out the sun's rays. In fact, there is nothing to say that you need curtains or blinds at all; often, a bare window makes more of a style statement than one that is shrouded in fabric. But if your room is overlooked, or if you feel the need for something at the window just to soften its outline, a plain blind or delicate curtains made of voile or muslin would be the best option. Keep the look simple by avoiding pelmets or ornate poles – café clips or tied

contemporary florals
look so fresh

this page It needs nothing more than a down-filled, coverless quilt to soften the lines of an old, unpolished wood bench and turn it into an inviting place to relax.

opposite, left
Instead of going to the trouble and expense of re-upholstering chairs, try wrapping them in generous lengths of linen tied at the back.

These are the quickest-to-make loose covers you have ever seen and look far less contrived than traditional upholstery.

opposite, right
Make the most of the decorative effect of your clothing and accessories. Silver shoes, left on view, have the power to make even this old staircase look elegant.

add surprising details then
simply relax

tab-tops to suspend the curtains project a much more relaxed and informal image.

To light your relaxed living room artificially, flexibility is the key. Have several pools of lamplight or candlelight rather than just one central light source and you will be able to light different corners of the room for different effects. The result will be far more soothing than light from a single source. Antique crystal-drop chandeliers, classic fifties Anglepoise lamps and even old industrial lights will all be perfectly at home. And with

relaxed living, there is no need to feel that the light fittings all have to match. In fact, an eclectic mixture of styles suits the mood better.

The colours you use on walls and ceilings will also have a bearing on the ambience you create in the living room. Good paint colours for a relaxed effect are neutral pale greens, beiges, greys, sky blues and off-whites, the latter offering more warmth and softness than that minimalists' favourite – pure, brilliant white.

Next, introduce splashes of brighter, more transient colour in the form of pictures, lampshades, vases and bowls, throws, rugs and

left This living room includes many of the ingredients of elegant living – a crystal chandelier, beautiful parquet flooring, an ornate overmantel, luxurious floor-length curtains and dramatic French windows. They have been put together so artlessly that they are the epitome of relaxed elegance.

opposite above, left and right Two very different mantelpiece arrangements show how idiosyncratic and eclectic even the smallest still life can be.

opposite below, left An enlarged photograph of a bunch of roses adds a note of femininity and romance to an otherwise simply decorated wall.

opposite below, right Loose covers, lots of soft cushions and a woollen throw quickly give a living area an easy, relaxed feel.

repose can come in
many guises

cushions – feather-filled for comfort, of course – then add to the sensual pleasure of the room by making as much use as possible of luxurious textured fabrics such as mohair, silk, velvet or leather. Supplement these with some satin-edged blankets or fringed pashmina shawls, then curling up on a chair or sofa or stretching out on the floor will be a truly sensual experience.

Dramatic touches of black – perhaps a black denim-covered beanbag, a large black and white photograph or a black and white ponyskin rug – can also work brilliantly in relaxed living rooms, provided they are used

sparingly. And if your preference is for a natural, organic look, this also has a place in the relaxed living room. Just make sure that you choose accessories in natural materials such as wood, stone, leather, terracotta, rattan, cane, rough linen and unbleached cotton to continue the organic theme.

Finally, remember that you do not have to stand on ceremony when it comes to decorating a relaxed living room. There is as

Minimalism meets hippy chic in a living room that owes its relaxed charm to the innovative mix of oriental fabrics and clean, contemporary furniture. Beautiful embroidered sari fabrics and cushions made from cotton combined with leather and Chinese embroidery soften the starkness of the upholstery and make the sofa cosy and inviting. Houseplants are enjoying something of a style revival and here they bring life and colour to the huge expanse of window. The rich tones of the polished wood floor add extra warmth and texture.

much scope for you to express your personality here as in any other part of the house. Bear in mind, too, that a living room that is truly relaxed does not require interior designing and careful matching of paint, accessory colours and fabrics. If you are too intense about it, you will end up with a room that is stuffy, over-decorated and precious, and you will have missed the point entirely.

Instead, you should just allow the room to evolve along the simplest of lines. Let it change to suit your moods, your needs and your lifestyle. Pick out one seriously comfortable sofa or chair, combine it with a beautiful, stylish and sensuous object or two, and you can give a sparse, simple room all the warmth, comfort and panache you could desire. With very little effort it will radiate an indubitably relaxed feel and your decoration will be true to yourself as well as in harmony with the rest of your home.

kitchens
and dining rooms

Place an honest-to-goodness kitchen next to
a simple yet stylish dining room, and
everything to do with food – its preparation
and eating – becomes totally relaxed.

It is often said that the kitchen is the heart of the home and should be the hub of family and social life. But the essence of the relaxed home is to allow your kitchen and dining area to meet your needs rather than your preconceptions. So while a kitchen that is cooking area, family meeting place and eating room, as well as the setting for more formal social gatherings, suits some households, it may not be what you require.

If you are something of a gourmet, then you will probably want to devote a whole room of your house to dining. For many people though, space restrictions mean that incorporating a table and chairs into the design of their kitchen is a more practical formula. It is one that can work just as well for a weekday family supper as for a dinner party with friends.

opposite Mismatched pieces of crockery, collected over the years, set just the right tone for a relaxed kitchen.

opposite (inset) An antique stencilled panel makes an unusual splashback that you could easily imitate.

right and below Unfitted kitchens maximize the space and feel relaxed. Here, side tables and an old-fashioned refrigerator provide essential storage. Only the sink cannot be moved.

When you have no choice but to put your table in the kitchen, it will have to be of the more workaday variety than a table standing in its own separate dining room. For inevitably, the kitchen dining table will sometimes have to serve as a work surface too. But forget the standard kitchen tables you can buy from department stores or furniture specialists. A tabletop made of bare planks resting on trestles or an old woodworking bench will suit the purpose admirably. Make sure that its top is not so vulnerable that hot pans and plates cannot be placed on top, and ensure it offers you a large enough surface, for in the relaxed home you will almost certainly want to be chopping vegetables at one end of the table while someone is writing a letter or making out the shopping list at the other.

Having a large, versatile work surface such as a kitchen table in the centre of your room

above left High
stools and an old
woodworking bench
create a relaxed
environment for
eating. Pale cream
paintwork lifts the
deep tones of the
furniture and the
terracotta floor.

above This room
owes its character to
an unusual selection
of mismatched chairs
and an eclectic
collection of rather
grand china. The
simple country table
brings everything
down to earth.

opposite, above
A beautiful collection
of gilded china adds
glamour to a kitchen,
but its opulence is
toned down by the
choice of an unfussy
white-painted display
cabinet.

opposite, below

In a country-style
kitchen with hints of
elegant living, a vase
full of casually
arranged fragrant
sweet peas ensures
that the sense of
simple relaxed country
life prevails.

86 relaxed rooms

there is no denying the fact that a kitchen is a place where food is prepared and served

is also part of the secret of creating a relaxed unfitted kitchen – one that is made up of freestanding pieces of furniture rather than rows of the usual built-in, made-to-measure units that have been popular for so many years. You might also like to have a trolley or a butcher's block in the kitchen. Either of these will provide you with extra space for food preparation, somewhere to stand hot pans when they come out of the oven, a place to hang towels and tea towels, and perhaps a drawer for storing small gadgets and kitchen knives.

Resisting the tyranny of the fitted kitchen means that you cannot hide away your food, crockery and utensils inside cupboards as you can with built-in units. The unfitted kitchen makes no pretence about being a place where food is prepared: it is much more honest than its fitted cousin. But do not worry that this will make it unattractive, for food and the paraphernalia of cooking can be decorative in their own right.

Put crockery, utensils and food stores boldly on show on open shelves, in cubby-holes, on stainless-steel shelving, hanging from hooks or displayed inside glass-fronted cabinets. Add glass jars filled with spices, bottles of oil and vinegar, packages of flour and sugar, containers to hold wooden spoons and spatulas, and stacks of cast-iron or copper pans.

Using lots of wood in the kitchen also helps to convey a sense of

opposite and below

From transforming a refrigerator door by covering it with black and white images to displaying crockery and utensils organized chaos is the keynote of these relaxed kitchens.

above Shop around for fittings with some originality. These old brass taps make the most of a workaday kitchen sink.

above right Building a kitchen from reclaimed timber gives it instant character and a collection of favourite photos adds individuality.

honesty and relaxation. With its many natural tones and textures, wood always has a restful effect and most other materials and colours look good with it too.

The taste for unfitted kitchens has brought a renewed interest in the look of kitchen appliances. For many years they were hidden away behind cupboard doors and decor panels. Their design became streamlined and co-ordinating – but sometimes a bit dull. Now though, there is a demand for the designs of the past – butlers' sinks with brass taps, old-fashioned refrigerators with curved casings and big chrome handles, food mixers with the distinctive retro look of the thirties and – that old rural favourite – the traditional kitchen range. Kitchen appliances have once again become focal points, rather than something to hide away.

the natural tones
of wood are restful
and timeless

But the streamlined look has its adherents and has undergone its own revolution. The result? Industrial chic, with kitchen appliances encased in chrome, stainless steel or brushed aluminium. Dishwashers, ovens and washing machines have become designer pieces in their own right. And so the wheel has turned full circle: these modern appliances, like their traditional counterparts, are seen and admired instead of being hidden away. Today's streamlined kitchens have a more honest feel than the streamlined kitchens that were fashionable twenty years ago.

above Dining thirties-style does not have to feel as formal as in those days. A nice relaxed touch is to only cover the dining table part-way, allowing the warm, honey tones of the wood to be appreciated. And instead of sticking strictly to period accessories, this collector has hung a stunning pair of working drawings by contemporary English sculptor Alan Grimwood on the walls.

above left This battered old tea tin and candles in a hand-carved wooden bowl could have been hidden away in a cupboard but instead they have become a decorative still life.

But whether you choose designer appliances in retro mode or with industrial-chic styling, you must be prepared to spend a little more on them than on conventional white goods. But it is a case of swings and roundabouts. If you are not going to the expense of installing a fitted kitchen and paying to hide appliances behind cupboards and matching fascias, you would instead do well to spend your money on acquiring better-looking well-designed kitchen basics.

As a backdrop to all this kitchen technology, it is best to keep the colours of the kitchen muted. Lots of white is always a winner and cannot fail to look clean and crisp, but a few soft pale colours can add a touch of prettiness.

opposite, left Here, an industrial steel bench is reinvented as an extra worktop in an unfitted kitchen.

opposite, right Create an utterly simple, totally relaxed decoration by stringing together some favourite objects and hanging them on a plain white wall.

above A simple kitchen display is nothing more than a row of silver mugs and a dangling scoop.

left The monastic feel of a dining room is softened by swathes of antique white linen and the abundance of light entering through elegant French windows.

However, if your kitchen does tend to be the hub of all household activity, a uniform colour scheme will help to unify the space and make it feel more peaceful.

The more neutral the decor, the fewer the restrictions when it comes to choosing crockery and glassware. In the relaxed kitchen, slavish style and colour co-ordination are a thing of the past. A mix-and-match approach will give the room a more carefree feel. Try sturdy Duralex tumblers alongside ornate gold-decorated porcelain, second-hand flowery plates from a flea market or wooden bowls brought back from a tropical holiday next to pure white plain china, chunky hand-thrown pots and plates alongside delicate Moroccan tea glasses. Forget purism. Once you have a relaxed kitchen, when you see a piece of glassware or a plate that you absolutely must have, you can buy it without worrying whether or not it will match.

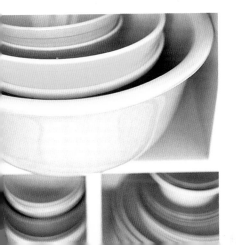

opposite Relaxed elegance is the main player in this dining room. Although on a large scale, the furniture is simple. Painting it to tone with the walls and woodwork removes any tendency towards excessive grandeur and helps to unify the space.

left Displays of vibrant ceramics and cutlery can be changed whenever you feel like it.

above Why not feel cheerful while you are washing the dishes? Canary yellow tiles bring a sense of fun to a small French kitchen, showing how colour can transform even the most restricted space.

right and opposite, left above Pale woods and white laminate dominate in this dining room. Introduce a hint of nature for a relaxing touch – a display of full-blown hydrangea heads and a contemporary piece of artwork consisting of individual ceramic panels united by their warm, natural earth colours.

opposite, left below Only with an eye for the relaxed eclectic look would one have the courage to combine the warm honey tones of an Art Deco dining suite with an industrial-style stainless-steel kitchen.

opposite, right A collection of unusual glass and ceramics displayed on an unconventional shelf unit adds a personal note to a minimalist kitchen/dining area.

When it comes to relaxed homes with the space for a separate dining room, there is even more scope for your imagination. For if you are lucky enough to have one, a separate dining room is where relaxed elegance can truly come into its own. Think generously sized tables, crisp tablecloths and ornate chairs. And there is no need to worry whether or not your accessories match. If anything, mismatched china, glassware and cutlery will help to create an easier-going atmosphere and you will feel more inclined to use the dining room on a regular, no-frills basis. Airy, neutral walls and

floors, fine linen, battered candelabra and a motley assortment of glassware – all these will defuse any tendency towards excessive formality while still imparting the glamour you want for special occasions.

Whether you have a separate dining room or a kitchen/diner, remember that you are more likely to focus on the delicious food and the company of family or friends if your surroundings are simple, stylish and thoroughly relaxed. Everything about the room where you sit down to eat should encourage you just to kick your shoes off under the table, eat your fill and enjoy.

bedrooms

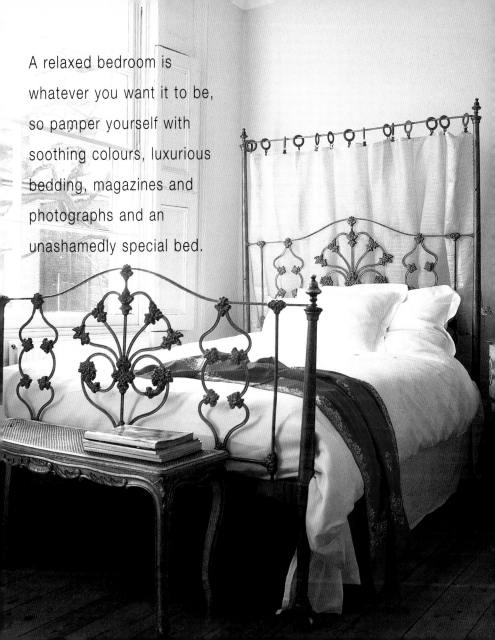

A relaxed bedroom is whatever you want it to be, so pamper yourself with soothing colours, luxurious bedding, magazines and photographs and an unashamedly special bed.

A lofty all-white room with old utilitarian metal lockers standing against one wall can be given just a hint of relaxed romance with understated floral pillowcases and a beautiful filmy throw, or perhaps with a sheer, floral curtain. The galvanized steel scaffolding poles of the bed and the severe, industrial bucket holding the flowers prevent both bed and flowers from being over-sentimental.

A bedroom is the most private space in the home, the one room you should be able to decorate as you like and fill with whatever makes you feel relaxed, happy and cosseted. For maximum relaxation, this usually means giving the bedroom a rather traditional ambience, using furniture that is familiar rather than innovative, bedding that is luxurious rather than spartan, colours that are soothing rather than invigorating.

A bedroom offers no shortage of opportunity to use a wealth of super-soft blankets, duvets, pillows, bolsters, quilts and eiderdowns. Do not stint on these – the more you put together and the more layered the finished effect, the more powerful the sense of ease and softness will be. During the colder months, put wool and mohair blankets on top of heavy feather-filled quilts, piling them all up on the bed in generous folds.

Then, when the weather warms up, swap them for crisply ironed linen sheets and subtly embroidered pillowslips layered with cool cotton bed covers and throws.

Complement this layered look by using plenty of fabrics elsewhere in the room, too. Fabrics at the window will help to cocoon you. Pick sheers in hot pinks and reds to cast a warm glow and make the space feel positively womb-like. Add a selection of contrasting fabrics for cushions, upholstery or bedspreads, and you will find yourself with some wonderful juxtapositions that can give the room unparalleled depth.

full of lightness and dreams

left and above An ornately carved four-poster bed has been painted white to blend with the painted brick-work of the walls. An eclectic collection of Asian fabrics and rose-sprigged pillowslips brings welcome colour.

You might end up with a gold-embroidered sari used as a throw on top of a mohair blanket; you could admire a fragile-looking floral pillowslip alongside a boldly printed viscose dress; you could place a beanbag covered in ethnic ikat beside a pile of old army blankets; you could drape a patchwork quilt over a batik sheet. Indulge your fancy, for this is relaxed eclecticism at its best.

And, instead of hanging all your clothing inside cupboards, add to the visual feast by placing favourite garments – anything from denim jackets and cocktail frocks to cotton shift dresses and cashmere cardigans – on pretty fabric-covered hangers and displaying them against a wall, suspended from the frame of a mirror, on a hook behind the door or just draped over the arm of a chair.

gorgeous beds take centre stage in simple surroundings

In another simple bedroom, the bed area is once again the room's welcoming focal point. In this case, an understated double bed is brought to life with a huge painting by the American artist Peter Zangrillo substituting for a headboard. An old American patchwork quilt covering the bed stands in sharp contrast to the painting, bringing together old and new strands of America's artistic heritage and adding a feeling of homely comfort. For those of us not fortunate enough to possess a work of art, a beautiful length of fabric or an alluring piece of vintage clothing could take pride of place over a bed in the same way.

left Write your diary in the privacy of your bedroom. Delicate flower-embroidered sheets make an eclectic mix with a journal covered in a bold, geometric-print fabric.

opposite, above and below left Why hide away lovely ethnic jewellery or beautiful fabrics spotted in an oriental bazaar? Here, Indian glass bangles grace a bedknob and a bolt of Chinese silk makes an eyecatching splash of colour on a chair. In a relaxed bedroom, the supporting cast is as important as the principal actors.

far right Delicately embroidered sheets and pillowcases, a gauzy pink curtain and a pair of Chinese silk slippers make a plain bedroom into an oasis of calm femininity where rest and relaxation prevail.

You can, if you like, do away with wardrobes altogether and simply hang your clothing on clothes rails so the clothing becomes part of the decor. But for open-plan storage such as this, bear in mind that sturdy wooden coat hangers are better looking than wire or plastic hangers, and make sure that your clothes are neat and tidy. And if you add a collection of beaded evening bags, some pieces of antique lace or a rack of strappy sequined sandals to your display, the effect will be even more unique and personal.

A collection of sixties furniture forms the basis for the decoration of this American apartment. The dark wood and laminate bedside table holds an unusual retro telephone and an angular fifties metal light fitting. The table stands on a clinical-looking pedestal on rubber feet. To prevent the room from looking like a museum piece, the owner has used an eyecatching piece of handblocked floral fabric as a throw on the bed.

Hiding beneath these richly built-up layers of clothing, bedding and accessories, the bedroom furniture you choose must include an unashamedly striking bed – perhaps a decadent four-poster in traditional or contemporary style, a nostalgic antique wrought-iron bedstead or showy brass bed, a bed constructed from starkly plain industrial scaffolding or an elegant bateau lit. Any one of these would make an imposing focal point and even a futon or the plainest low-lying divan would lack nothing in terms of comfort if you set it against plain walls and deck it out in the simplest starched white bedlinen.

Mirrors are another essential, increasing the amount of light and giving the room a dream-like quality. You will certainly want a small mirror for putting on make-up, but when it comes to seeing yourself full length, choose the largest mirror you can find and give it the relaxed treatment by standing it on the floor rather than hanging it on the wall or hiding it away inside a cupboard door. For a touch of glamour choose a mirror with an ornately carved natural or gilded wood frame: for a simpler effect, keep the mirror as plain as plain can be. Either way, you will want it on show.

Maintain the sense of light and space by keeping your colour scheme simple and based on pastel colours, using sky blues, powder pinks, gentle lilacs, pale turquoises and white. Window treatments should be as minimalist as possible. Avoid heavy curtains and if your bedroom is overlooked, consider using Venetian blinds or muslin panels. These strike just the right balance between providing privacy and allowing daylight in.

Add the rest of your bedroom furnishings according to your needs and the available

A soft honeycomb-weave throw adds a flash of bright colour and a sense of cosiness to a masculine, almost monastic room.

opposite, left Even a small collection of eclectic retro pieces on a mantelshelf can be a talking point.

opposite, right The owners of this thirties apartment have taken the style of the building as the starting point for their interior decoration. Louvre blinds and a chunky glass-fronted bookcase suit its mood but the modern vases and cardboard-covered drum add hints of individuality.

space. Rather than sticking to the conventional dressing-table-and-wardrobe formula, it is more original – and very relaxed – to borrow from other parts of the house. Import a shabby chic armchair from your living room to provide you with a comfortable place to sit and read a book in peace at any time of the day. Hat stands, usually seen exclusively in hallways, make perfect makeshift clothes horses, while old school lockers, more often filled with junk and standing dully in a utility room, double up as brilliantly unconventional wardrobes. Prop up a large oil painting behind a divan in place of a bedhead. Use open shelf units

fill your bedroom with

whatever makes you happy

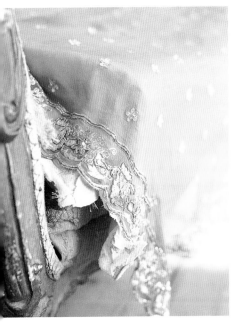

**opposite and above
right** There is no
better room to turn
into a haven of
sensousness than the
bedroom. Here wood,
cane, crisp bedlinens,
straw baskets, antique
lace and embroidery
and gold-encrusted
Indian shawls combine
as if without a care in
the world.

left and above left
For glamour and
elegance drape a
sheer, gold-trimmed
sari over an old sofa.

above Hand-me-
down shop fittings
make unusual storage
for bedrooms.

from the kitchen to display your shoes and bags. Hang jewellery from old dressmakers' dummies, string it around decorative lampshades or pile it high in pretty china dishes. Fill a shopping basket with scarves and gloves and stand it on the floor or on a small table.

The secret is to think laterally, remembering that a bedroom does not have to be only a bedroom. If you blur the boundaries a little, it can become part-boudoir, part-dressing room, part-private sitting room. Collections of books, magazines, paintings, plants and photographs find a home where once there were only clothes and toiletries. Include piles of paperbacks here and there, line shelves with framed snapshots, hang your favourite artwork on walls and decorate windowsills with anything from rows of pretty glass perfume bottles to pots of geraniums.

Implement just a few of these ideas and you will create the perfect relaxed bedroom, somewhere you will want to linger during daylight instead of only retreating to at night.

top Make a cool bedroom feel welcoming with a sumptuous, velvet-trimmed bedspread.

above left and right Revel in the unusual juxtaposition of a utilitarian desk lamp and a seventies light fitting with a completely over-the-top carved wooden bed. These are the type of surprising combinations that relaxed eclectic makes possible.

opposite You can easily personalize an all-white bedroom simply by pegging family photographs around the room on lengths of thin wire. Beautiful turquoise bedlinen adds colour, warmth and romance.

bathrooms

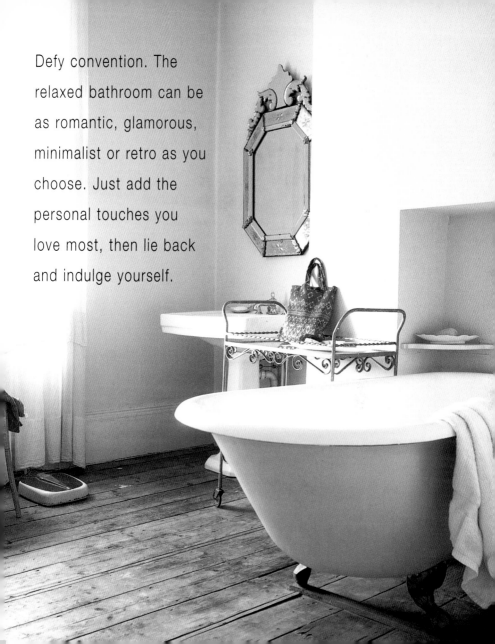

Defy convention. The relaxed bathroom can be as romantic, glamorous, minimalist or retro as you choose. Just add the personal touches you love most, then lie back and indulge yourself.

Decorating your bathroom gives you the chance to create a haven of relaxation, a place where you can just soak away your stresses and strains. But to make the room as therapeutic as possible – and to maintain the spirit of relaxed living – you need to include some deeply personal touches. Only you can know which details will help you unwind and feel at ease, so close your eyes and imagine your most perfectly restful bathroom.

above Chunky antique chrome taps and an unusual plug device make an eyecatching addition to a plain white washbasin.

right and opposite This bathroom captures the spirit of bathtimes past and a sense of the beauty to be found in utility. The star turn is the freestanding, rolltop bath. The shelf unit, bathroom scales and wooden bench convey a similar effect.

If the image you conjure up is one of femininity and glamour, you should have some floral patterns and soft fabrics in your bathroom alongside the usual fixtures and fittings. Warm up the ubiquitous white of the room with colours such as strong, hot pinks or vivacious turquoises. Let everyone know how much you love life's pleasures by lining your bathroom shelves with your favourite toiletries and cosmetics displayed in old glass bottles and jars or in a selection of bowls and baskets.

Alternatively, your perfect bathroom might be altogether simpler, possibly even verging on the austere and monastic. This is a place where there is nothing to distract you from the ritual of cleansing mind and body. Wetrooms – essentially open-plan, completely waterproofed spaces – are the simplest bathrooms of all. For these you need a floor that slopes gently so the water can drain away, waterproof walls, a powerful shower and some basic, hardworking accessories such as big blocks of soap, natural sponges and loofahs.

use gauzy curtains for a
touch of glamour

far left and left
Create a retro-style
bathroom with brick-
shaped tiles, an old
shower fitting and
accessories such as
these bathroom scales.

below Crisp linen
towels are piled on an
old dentist's cabinet.

opposite Sheer
beaded curtains bring
colour and glamour to a
monochrome bathroom.

Some people find that a sleek modern
bathroom is what they need to feel at ease.
These bathrooms make the most of materials
such as concrete, glass and stainless steel;
they have an almost industrial feel to them. If
this is the look that appeals to you, choose
features such as stainless steel or stone sinks,
chrome designer taps or sandblasted glass
shower screens. The plainer the details, the
better, but to make the effect just a little softer
and more relaxed, try adding a pile of fluffy
towels, or a single flower in a glass vase.

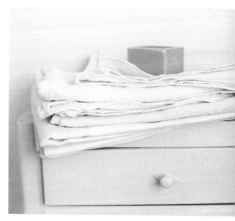

Alternatively, you may long to create a bathroom with a retro feel, faithfully using reclaimed fittings to hark back in time. Old tiles, metal-framed bathroom shelves, ornate, solidly made taps and shower fittings, chunky chrome towel rails, a set of old-fashioned bathroom scales – all give a sense of the bathtimes enjoyed by the comfortable middle classes of a hundred or so years ago.

In a retro bathroom, aim to give the space the sort of honesty that is so often lacking in modern, fitted bathrooms, where everything

above Although this bathroom has a sense of the past, it is not a museum piece. Painting the walls blue, the outside of the bath black and the woodwork and floor white brings it up to date. The textured cotton rug adds some softness.

above right An alcove makes an attractive bathroom display area. Matching chrome-lidded storage jars hold bathroom necessities, while the brown tones of a seashell collection complement a bowl of wooden-handled toothbrushes.

far left and left

All-white walls and ceiling form the backdrop to this small Parisian bathroom which is also a wetroom. Dispensing with the usual shower screen or curtain means that there is greater flexibility in the use of the space. The floor, sloping gently towards a drain in the centre of the room and covered with bold blue and beige tiles, is the focal point.

is hidden away behind panels or inside integral units. Achieve this freer look by following the principle that there is beauty in utility – in other words, revel in the bold designs of the hardware of the past. You could start by installing a big, freestanding, cast-iron, roll-top bath in pride of place in the centre of the room. Or indulge yourself with an old-fashioned mixer tap or a dinner plate-sized showerhead. You might even find the courage to leave your bathroom's pipework on show instead of boxing it all in.

Do not worry that this honest, practical approach will mean that you have to sacrifice your comfort. In the early days of plumbed-in baths, bathrooms were, by modern standards, huge. This meant that baths and wash basins were also on the generous side, so if you are used to bathing in the cramped conditions of today, you will find old sanitary ware extremely practical. Nothing is more relaxing than to be able to stretch out in a deep turn-of-the-century bath. What is more, you can personalize your bath by painting its

A hint of wood, some pale ochre-coloured tiles, a few fluffy towels and some bottles and jars just visible through a frosted glass panel make a stark bathroom feel more welcoming.

soft fluffy towels and favourite photographs
meet minimalism

exterior – black for impact, white for simplicity, cream for classic restraint. The feet of the bath can also tell a story: choose ball-and-claw feet for total authenticity or streamlined chrome for a more unexpected combination.

As with the relaxed bedroom, there is no reason why your bathroom should not borrow pieces of furniture or accessories from other rooms in the house – perhaps an armchair from the living room, an ornate trolley from the dining room, a coat rack from the hall. Any of these additions would lend a relaxed, uniquely personal character to your bathroom and will prevent it from looking as if it has just stepped from the sterile, lifeless pages of a sanitary ware catalogue.

For the floor, simple flooring looks best and is most practical. Bare floorboards are easy to clean, but make them more user-friendly with the addition of a plain white cotton rug. The modern bathroom needs something more refined underfoot – perhaps marble or terrazzo – while for the industrial-looking bathroom, concrete flooring is the preferred accompaniment. Linoleum is back in fashion and is once again being manufactured in a wide range of colours and designs. It is the perfect choice for retro bathrooms. A further flooring option comes in the shape of ceramic tiles, which can be used to create no end of special effects, from the subtle decorative qualities of encaustic insets

With plain white walls and an unfinished concrete floor as a starting point, the owner of this bathroom could easily have taken its decoration in the direction of minimalism. Instead, the simple background has been given an injection of romance and femininity. The use of a single rose-printed cotton curtain gently filtering the light from the large window, and a glassful of flowers creates a look that is fresh and utterly charming. The sense of light is magnified by the large thirties mirror over the washbasin, while the freestanding roll-top bath adds a leisured feel.

industrial chic
and delicate florals
create an air of
romance

to the clean, clinical look of glazed tiles in purest, plainest white.

If you want to give an existing bathroom a relaxed makeover, there are many simple ways of doing it. Try covering the walls with tongue-and-groove panelling painted in white or gently muted pink, blue or green to ensure the room feels spacious and airy. Glass shelves are perfect, too. As well as bringing a sense of light to a bathroom, they provide valuable and practical storage space. And instead of a dull, standard bathroom mirror, try finding an old mirror. It does not need to have a beautiful gilded antique frame or a spectacular Venetian-glass frame – although either of these would, of course, be lovely. Any unusual, old, well-proportioned mirror will catch the eye and make your bathroom that little bit different.

In a similar vein, an antique washstand makes a lovely perch for a pile of towels, some natural sponges and other bathtime treats. And instead of putting your soap in a standard soap dish, try the more relaxed effect of using a favourite china bowl, perhaps one large enough to hold several soaps from which you can choose according to your mood. And finally, do not forget flowers. The bathroom is one room we often forget to decorate with flowers, but a small, simple arrangement will go a long way towards creating an atmosphere that verges tantalizingly on the sybaritic.

It can be as simple as this to make a relaxed bathroom that is as glamorous and distinctive as the rest of your home. Most of the work has been done for you for many of the good things in life – plenty of hot running water, piles of soft towels and your favourite toiletries – are probably already in place. The rest is only a short step away.

workrooms

A comfortable
workspace means a
creative worker, so
make your home
office relaxing, turn
your back on standard-
issue office furniture
and feed your senses
while you work.

sugar-almond

colours defy convention

More and more people are choosing to work from home instead of commuting to a faceless office every day. But even if you are not a fully-fledged home-worker, you probably still need a home work station. Use some of the following simple ideas, and there is no reason why this space should not become as relaxed and stylish as the rest of your home.

The first rule is, get personal. To maximize your creativity, you need to be comfortable and surrounded by some of your favourite things. No one is at their best working in cramped conditions and surrounded by bland walls and anonymous office equipment. So rather than a mass-produced office desk, start with a simple trestle table, an old-fashioned bureau or a pine refectory table.

Next, you need a comfortable chair that is ergonomically suited to the work you do. Instead of a standard-issue office chair, choose one you really like – perhaps a Charles Eames design classic, a padded dining chair, or an antique office clerk's chair. If you like, dress it up with a new cover and, to add a sense of fun and irreverence, choose an unusual material, one not usually seen in a work environment – fake fur, faded chintz, jazzy vinyl or raw linen.

A touch of humour will also help make your room feel less like a conventional workspace. Use a dressmaker's dummy to pin notes on or make a pinboard for anything that will inspire you as you work – postcards, magazine cuttings, fabric swatches, photos.

opposite, above An ingenious cupboard doubles as desk and office storage.

opposite, below Be carried far away from the world of work with a desk made from a white-painted pasting table and unexpected, lilac-painted walls.

above right An alcove fitted with shelves makes an ideal place to store box files.

above far right With careful planning you can arrange the tools of your trade so they are aesthetically pleasing.

below right Surround yourself with good-looking office equipment like these notebooks and paperweight.

below far right These matching box files also create blocks of colour that help to unify the space.

Once you have stamped your personality on your workroom, you need a degree of order and discipline to make it work well and ensure that your stress levels do not escalate as you struggle to locate a file or find a document. So some sort of filing system is essential, but why be conventional?

Shoeboxes covered in pretty fabrics or old hat boxes or trunks can provide the organization you need and are very attractive. You could try colour co-ordinating the smaller elements – blue for household bills, yellow for professional accounts, and so on.

above right and opposite A fashion designer who works from home finds inspiration in a wall covered from top to bottom with magazine and newspaper cuttings, fabric swatches – even plastic bags and soap packaging.

centre and below right Even if your taste in office decoration veers towards the minimalist, you can loosen up and relax a little by adding a couple of roses in a glass to a shelf full of useful books.

left The home office for the person who likes clarity of thought. A polished concrete floor and blank walls are brought to life with a no-nonsense red leather chair.

who says work cannot be

creative?

opposite A modern chair contrasts with an old scrubbed-pine table in an office where you can stay cool, calm and collected whatever your schedule. Work is stored beneath the desk in boxes draped casually with linen towels, while candles on the table add a period note.

this page A sense of unity is maintained in this busy home workspace by sticking to a simple scheme of white and natural wood.

this page (inset) Keep some much-loved possessions nearby to remind you of life beyond work.

Other low-tech storage, such as a selection of old tins in place of standard plastic pen holders, makes a humorous contrast with the fax machine, phone and computer. With touches such as these, there is never the risk that the room will be overtaken by soulless plastic.

If you cannot dedicate a whole room to your office but have to work in a corner of another room, you might consider a large cupboard combining desk and storage space. Alternatively, hunt out an old, all-concealing rolltop desk or screen off the area with an attractive room divider.

Whatever kind of workspace you need, get the balance right between discipline and freedom, and any work you have to do will seem much more enjoyable.

above Decorate your workspace with images of friends and family.

right Influences from different places and eras make a home office area that is totally relaxed. Here a pierced metal lamp from North Africa sits alongside a retro desk lamp and a more modern phone, clock and photographs.

opposite A velvet-covered seat turns a utilitarian tubular metal chair into a relaxing place to sit.

opposite, below left and right A desk lamp for good light is essential. Do away with conventional office storage.

outdoors

Combine beautiful plants
and easy-going furniture
in relaxed outdoor
spaces, then feel the
healing power of nature
and beat the stress.

In today's hi-tech world, people live life at a hectic pace. To help us relax, many of us need to re-establish some link, however small, with nature. By creating an outdoor room or other space that blurs the boundaries between outside and in, you can benefit from the healing powers of nature without even leaving the confines of your home.

You do not need to have a large garden to achieve this. Your outdoor room could just as easily be a conservatory, the tiniest back yard, a sunny verandah, a lean-to shed, a shady porch or simply a room with large French windows. If you are really short of space, your link with nature need be nothing more than a collection of windowboxes or some flower pots by the front door.

To give your outdoor room the same unique style as the rest of your house, treat it just as you would any other room. Make it relaxed and natural and remember to choose furniture and accessories that you really love. To start with, you do not need to buy expensive new garden furniture. One of the delights of relaxed living is to discover that modestly priced rattan furniture and junk-shop finds

left Never mind that you only have a porch as your outdoor space. Be relaxed about it, take a huge, comfortable chair from the living room whenever the sun shines, sit back and enjoy.

right You do not need special furniture for a relaxed outdoor space. A simple folding chair

makes a perfect perch for pots filled with summer plants.

far right Place a simple wooden bench on a wide verandah so you can sit outside whenever you feel the urge. All you need add in order to feel completely relaxed is a soft flower-covered cushion.

are even more at home outdoors than in.
If you can find them, pieces such as daybeds
and steamer chairs will always add a relaxed,
languorous air, but if there is no room to
keep more than the odd tiny, rickety garden
chair outdoors, then do not worry. When
the weather turns fine, simply take a small,
comfortable armchair and some soft
cushions from the living room and sit
and enjoy.

Roughly finished wooden furniture is
another excellent choice for your outdoor
room. Its earthiness will help you feel more

above left and right
Give foliage
houseplants the
relaxed treatment with
a huge gilt mirror
propped up among
them and some exotic
accessories.

right What could look
more relaxed than
these fifties cane chairs
set in a tiny wood-
floored roof garden
against a wall of
terracotta tiles?

opposite, right If
outdoor space is at a
premium, simply open
the door and relax in an
old metalwork chair with
pot plants at your feet.
A delicate chandelier
adds a charming yet
elegant touch.

opposite, left The
chaise longue comes
up to date to provide
the ultimate in
sophisticated
relaxation.

in touch with nature. Accessorize with plenty of terracotta pots, basketware, ethnic textiles and, for indoor/outdoor spaces, unvarnished wood floors. Or, if you prefer more elegance, masses of tropical plants accompanied by dark wood furniture and swathes of sheer fabric, mosquito-net style, add colonial grandeur.

Sensuality plays a large part in the enjoyment of any outdoor space. Revel in the sight and texture of your plants, whether a collection of luscious houseplants, troughs of flowering annuals or a selection of evergreens. Scented plants add another dimension to one's enjoyment, especially in conservatories, where the warmth heightens their fragrance. And if a conservatory is out of the question, fill

a room with intoxicating scent by planting a honeysuckle or jasmine outside a window, or by putting some aromatic herbs in a windowbox on the windowsill.

Besides enjoying these sights and smells, you will find that tending your plants is a fantastic stress-buster. And caring for your outdoor space will give you an outlet for your nurturing and creative skills as well as being a constructive way to spend your time. With an outdoor room that is as relaxed as the rest of your house, nothing will be able to spoil your tranquillity.

stockists and suppliers

Laura Ashley
t. 020 7880 5100 for branches
www.lauraashley.com
Fabric, furniture and accessories

Bennisons Fabrics
16 Holbein Place
London SW1W 8NL
t. 020 730 8076
www.bennisonsfabrics.com
Traditional floral fabrics

Borovick Fabrics
16 Berwick Street
London W1F 0HP
t. 020 7437 0520
www.borovickfabricsltd.co.uk
Range of fabrics for the stage

Carden Cunietti
83 Westbourne Park Road
London W2 5QH
t. 020 7229 8630
www.carden-cunietti.com
Interior design shop mixing old
and new

The Cloth Shop
290 Portobello Road
London W10 5TE
t. 020 8968 6001
www.clothshop.net
Fabrics

Cornucopia
12 Upper Tachbrook Street
London SW1V 1SH
t. 020 7828 5752
Vintage clothing store

Country Colonials
t. 020 7723 0465 for stockists
Fabric accessories for the
home with an Eastern theme

The Cross
141 Portland Road
London W11 4LR
t. 020 7727 6760
Eclectic haven of girly fashion
and home products

Decorative Living
55 New Kings Road
London SW6 4SE
t. 020 7736 5623
www.decorativeliving.co.uk
Antiques

Nicole Farhi Home Collection
17 Clifford Street
London W1S 3RQ
t. 020 7494 9051
www.nicolefarhi.com
Old and new home accessories

Joss Graham
10 Eccleston Street
London SW1W 9LT
t. 020 7730 4370
Clothes and objects from India,
Africa and the Far East

Graham & Green
4–10 Elgin Crescent
London W11 2HX
t. 0845 1306622
www.grahamandgreen.co.uk
Established west London
interiors shop

Judy Greenwood Antiques
659 Fulham Road
London SW6 5PY
t. 020 7736 6037
www.judygreenwoodantiques.
co.uk
Antique French furniture

Cath Kidston
8 Clarendon Cross
London W11 4AP
t. 020 7221 4000
www.cathkidston.co.uk
Fabrics and interiors with
a retro feel

Liberty
Regent Street
London W1B 5AH
t. 020 7734 1234
www.liberty.co.uk
Fantastic fabrics

Andrew Martin
200 Walton Street
London SW3 2JL
t. 020 7225 5100
www.andrewmartin.co.uk
Modern fabric and furniture

Mark Maynard
651 Fulham Road
London SW6 5PU
t. 020 7731 3533
www.markmaynard.co.uk
Antique shop specialising in
painted furniture

MacCulloch & Wallis
25–26 Dering Street
London W1S 1AT
t. 020 7629 0311
www.macculloch-wallis.co.uk
Huge range of fabrics and
haberdashery

Minh Mang
Battersea Park Road
London SW11 4ND
t. 020 7498 3233
www.minhmang.co.uk
Chinese and Vietnamese
fashion and interiors
accessories

Pimpernel & Partners
596 Kings Road
London SW6 2DX
t. 020 7731 2448
Antiques

Retro Home
56 Notting Hill Gate
London W11 3HT
t. 020 7792 3474
20th-century furniture
and accessories

Sandersons
Sanderson House
Oxford Road
Denham UB9 4DX
t. 01895 830044
www.sandersons-uk.com
Fabrics, wallpaper and paints

SCP Furniture
135–139 Curtain Road
London EC2A 3BX
t. 020 7739 1869
www.scp.co.uk
British modern furniture design
at its best

Summerill & Bishop
100 Portland Road
London W11 4LN
t. 020 7221 4566
Kitchen accessories and
furniture, specialising in French
products

Toast
t. 01558 668800 Mail order
www.toastbypost.co.uk
Fashion and home accessories

Tobias And The Angel
68 White Hart Lane
London SW13 0PZ
t. 020 8878 8902
www.tobiasandtheangel.com
Antique furniture and accessories

Viaduct Furniture
1–10 Summer's Street
London EC1R 5BD
t. 020 7278 8456
www.viaduct.co.uk
Classic modern furniture

Whaleys (BFD)
Harris Court
Great Horton
Bradford BD7 4EQ
t. 01274 576718
www.whaleys-bradford.ltd.uk
Huge range of plain fabrics

picture credits

Key: t = top, b = below, l = left, r = right, c = centre

Endpapers Clare Nash's house in London; **1** Mary Foley's house in Connecticut; **2–3** Adria Ellis' apartment in New York; **6** Clare Nash's house in London; **7 l** Ann Shore's former home in London; **7 c** Mary Foley's house in Connecticut; **7 r** Daniel Jasiak's apartment in Paris; **8 l & c** Liz Stirling's apartment in Paris; **8 r** Ann Shore's former home in London; **9** Kathy Moskal's apartment in New York designed by Ken Foreman; **12–13** Louise Jackson's house in London; **14–15** Clare Nash's house in London; **16** Kathy Moskal's apartment in New York designed by Ken Foreman; **18 l** Clare Nash's house in London; **18 r** Ann Shore's former home in London; **19** Daniel Jasiak's apartment in Paris; **20** Ros Fairman's house in London; **21** Mary Foley's house in Connecticut; **22 l** an apartment in New York designed by Belmont Freeman Architects; **25 t** Lena Proudlock's house in Gloucestershire; **26** Ros Fairman's house in London; **27 tl & br** Ros Fairman's house in London; **27 tr** Adria Ellis' apartment in New York; **29** Ann Shore's former home in London; **30 & 30–31** Kimberley Watson's house in London; **31 r** Ros Fairman's house in London; **32 l** Liz Stirling's apartment in Paris; **32 r & 33** Ann Shore's

former home in London; **34, 35 tl & br** Liz Stirling's apartment in Paris; **36** Ann Shore's former home in London; **37** Daniel Jasiak's apartment in Paris; **38** Carol Reid's apartment in Paris; **39 tl** Glenn Carwithen & Sue Miller's house in London; **39 b** Carol Reid's apartment in Paris; **40–41 & 42** Ros Fairman's house in London; **43** Clare Nash's house in London; **44** Marie-Hélène de Taillac's pied-à-terre in Paris; **46 tr** Kimberley Watson's house in London; **47** Marie-Hélène de Taillac's pied-à-terre in Paris; **48 bl** Home of 27.12 Design Ltd., Chelsea, NYC; **48 r & 49** Glenn Carwithen & Sue Miller's house in London; **50 & 51 bl** Home of 27.12 Design Ltd., Chelsea, NYC; **51 tr & br** an apartment in New York designed by Belmont Freeman Architects; **52–53** The Sawmills Studios; **54–55** Marie-Hélène de Taillac's pied-à-terre in Paris; **56–57** Glenn Carwithen & Sue Miller's house in London; **58 l** Glenn Carwithen & Sue Miller's house in London; **58 r & 59** Mary Foley's house in Connecticut; **60 l** Courtney Brennan's apartment in New York designed by Ken Foreman; **60 r & 61** an apartment in New York designed by Belmont Freeman Architects; **62** Kathy Moskal's apartment in New York designed by Ken Foreman; **63 l**

an apartment in New York designed by Belmont Freeman Architects; **63 tr** Kathy Moskal's apartment in New York designed by Ken Foreman; **64** Louise Jackson's house in London; **65** Lena Proudlock's house in Gloucestershire; **66–67** Carol Reid's apartment in Paris; **68** Clare Nash's house in London; **69 tl & b** Kimberley Watson's house in London; **69 tc** Daniel Jasiak's apartment in Paris; **69 tr** Clare Nash's house in London; **70 l & 71 tl** Clare Nash's house in London; **70 r & 71 r** Mary Foley's house in Connecticut; **72 l** Adria Ellis' apartment in New York; **73** The Sawmills Studios; **74 & 75 l** Daniel Jasiak's apartment in Paris; **75 r** Ann Shore's former home in London; **76** Daniel Jasiak's apartment in Paris; **77 tl** Adria Ellis' apartment in New York; **77 tr** Kimberley Watson's house in London; **77 bl & br** Mary Foley's house in Connecticut; **78–79** Kimberley Watson's house in London; **80–81** Glenn Carwithen & Sue Miller's house in London; **82 l** Louise Jackson's house in London; **82 r** Lena Proudlock's house in Gloucestershire; **83** The Sawmills Studios; **84–85** Ros Fairman's house in London; **86 tl & br** Ann Shore's former home in London; **86 tr, c & bl** Clare Nash's house in London; **86 bc** Daniel Jasiak's

apartment in Paris; **87** Ann Shore's former home in London; **88** Carol Reid's apartment in Paris; **89 l & br** Ann Shore's former home in London; **89 tr** Glenn Carwithen & Sue Miller's house in London, painting by Alan Grimwood; **90 l** The Sawmills Studios; **90 r & 91** Daniel Jasiak's apartment in Paris; **92** Lena Proudlock's house in Gloucestershire; **93 l & br** Home of 27.12 Design Ltd., Chelsea, NYC; **93 tr** Marie-Hélène de Taillac's pied-à-terre in Paris; **93 cr** Adria Ellis' apartment in New York; **94** Courtney Brennan's apartment in New York designed by Ken Foreman; **95 t** Kimberley Watson's house in London; **95 b** an apartment in New York designed by Belmont Freeman Architects; **96–97** Ros Fairman's house in London; **98–99** The Sawmills Studios; **100** Mary Foley's house in Connecticut; **101** Adria Ellis' apartment in New York, painting by Peter Zangrillo; **103** Kimberley Watson's house in London; **104–105** an apartment in New York designed by Belmont Freeman Architects; **106** Home of 27.12 Design Ltd., Chelsea, NYC; **107** Glenn Carwithen & Sue Miller's house in London; **108** Ann Shore's former home in London; **109 bl & c** Ros Fairman's house in London;

ARCHITECTS AND DESIGNERS WHOSE WORK HAS BEEN FEATURED IN THIS BOOK

Ken Foreman
Architect
105 Duane Street
New York, NY 10007
USA
t/f +1 212 924 4503
Pages 9, 16, 60 l, 62, 63 tr, 94, 120, 128 tr, cr & br, 129

Belmont Freeman Architects
Project team: Belmont Freeman (Principal Designer), Alane Truitt, Sangho Park
110 West 40th Street
New York, NY 10018
USA
t. +1 212 382 3311
f. +1 212 730 1229
Pages 22 l, 51 tr & br, 60 r, 61, 63 l, 95 b, 104–105, 120–121, 128 l

Jacksons
5 All Saints Road
London W11 1HA
t. 020 7792 8336
Pages 12–13, 64, 82 l, 110 bl & br

Daniel Jasiak
Designer
12 rue Jean Ferrandi
Paris 75006 France
t. +33 (0)1 45 49 13 56
f. +33 (0)1 45 49 23 66
Pages 7 r, 19, 37, 69 tc, 74, 75 l, 76, 86 bc, 90 r, 91, 131 tl & r, 132 c & r, 133

Lena Proudlock
Denim in Style
Drews House, Leighterton
Gloucestershire GL8 8UN
t/f 01666 890230
www.deniminstyle.com
Pages 25 t, 65, 82 r, 92, 111, 114 b, 115, 118 l, 126 b, 127 tl & tr

Ann Shore
London-based Designer, Stylist and Owner of Story
4 Wilkes Street
London E1 6QF
t. 020 7377 0313
story@btconnect.com
Pages 7 l, 8 r, 18 r, 29, 32 r, 33, 36, 75 r, 86 tl & br, 87, 89 l & br, 108, 109 tr, 130, 131 bl, 132 l, 136–137, 138–139

27.12 Design Ltd.
333 Hudson Street,
10th Floor
New York, NY 10014
USA
t. +1 212 727 8169
www.2712design.com
Pages 48 bl, 50, 51 bl, 93 l & br, 106

index

acknowledgements

Firstly I would like to say a huge thank you to Polly Wreford for her dedication
and visual insight; for consistently taking such exquisite pictures and for keeping
us all smiling with her infectious laugh. Also, thanks to Matt Wrixon for his good
humour and hard work, and of course to Gloria Daniel for her boundless energy
and support. I could not have wished for a better team.

Thanks to Alice Westgate for her unfailing assistance in ensuring the text was
written on time and to everyone at Ryland Peters & Small, especially Ann Ryland
and Gabriella Le Grazie for giving me such a wonderful opportunity. I would also
like to thank Kate Brunt and Hilary Mandleberg for their much-needed help and
Vicky Holmes for the book's beautiful design.

But most of all thanks to Dave for his inspiration, encouragement and for
generally being fantastic.